How to Kill a Goat &
Other Monsters

WISCONSIN POETRY SERIES

Sean Bishop and Jesse Lee Kercheval, *series editors*
Ronald Wallace, *founding series editor*

How to Kill a Goat & Other Monsters

Saúl Hernández

THE UNIVERSITY OF WISCONSIN PRESS

Publication of this book has been made possible, in part, through support from the Brittingham Trust.

The University of Wisconsin Press
728 State Street, Suite 443
Madison, Wisconsin 53706
uwpress.wisc.edu

Gray's Inn House, 127 Clerkenwell Road
London EC1R 5DB, United Kingdom
eurospanbookstore.com

Printed in the United States of America
This book may be available in a digital edition.

Library of Congress Cataloging-in-Publication Data

Names: Hernández, Saúl, 1989– author.
Title: How to kill a goat & other monsters / Saúl Hernández.
Other titles: How to kill a goat and other monsters | Wisconsin poetry series.
Description: Madison, Wisconsin : The University of Wisconsin Press, 2024. | Series: Wisconsin poetry series
Identifiers: LCCN 2023040074 | ISBN 9780299347840 (paperback)
Subjects: LCGFT: Poetry.
Classification: LCC PS3608.E7678 H69 2024 | DDC 811/.6—dc23/eng/20231013
LC record available at https://lccn.loc.gov/2023040074

Para mis padres, SanJuana Hernandez Ibarra y Arturo Alvarez Hernandez.

Y para todos los padres indocumentados.

& for all the LGBTQIA+ individuals—I see you.

& for anyone who has lived for a dream.

I want to be
like the waves on the sea,
like the clouds in the wind,
but I'm me.
One day I'll jump
out of my skin.
I'll shake the sky
like a hundred violins.

—SANDRA CISNEROS, *The House on Mango Street*

Contents

How to Kill a Goat &
Other Monsters

In Another Life

My parents never left México,

I never learned to open my mouth. Gnats circle me in the milpa, my sandpaper hands pull another tomato off a vine. I raise the tomato up to the sky, crush it, let the juice run down my hand.

How easy it is to be ripe & not ready.

I'm in love with a woman from the next town over. On the weekdays, I make love to men who look at me with hunger. Their knuckles pop against my back when they squeeze me. Mosquitoes bite us in the fields, remind us how our blood rises the most with things

you cannot have.

The day I marry her, in the only church in town, I wait for her at the altar with the head of my lover as a gesture of my loyalty. I pluck out his teeth, petals I blow to her, & tell her: *¿Quién te quiere un chingo?*

On our first night together, she cuts my tongue out, makes guisado out of it. *You don't need to be kissing me*, she tells me. When she eats my tongue she tastes all the men I had before her. *This guisado is too salty.* She adds honey, serves me a plate, & peels my tongue apart with a fork. After dinner, she flosses my teeth with a strand of her hair.

The next day, when I open my mouth to kiss a man in the fields, flies buzz out of me. The man steps back, *Con esa boca nadie te va a querer.* I put my head down, pull tomatoes off vines, collect them in my bag like the lovers I'll never have in either lifetime.

First Wave

The Boy Who Lives in Dreams

Dreams run in my family. In mine, I
    nail water to the wall, it runs down

my hands & splashes at my feet, leaks
    into the cracks of the hardwood floor. In

the morning, I wash my face, water
    goes down my elbows &

drips. I hear the water in the sink ask
    me: *I need to know your*

dreams. Apá fights at night. I can hear
    him toss & groan. He knows where

sleep will take him: to see his brother
    drown. I take sleeping pills sometimes

to become heavy enough to not
    dream. Like when Amá puts Valium pills in her

mouth, keeping her father from telling her:
    Why didn't you come bury me? When it rains,

I have to remember I'm awake, not dreaming.
    Water remembers its path, always forming

the same stream, moving in the same direction, like
    the way my body waits at night:

always still, sweating out the night.
  I can hear heavy drops slam against the floor. I

get up, open the cracks of the wood floor,
    take a shovel, scoop up all the water that has leaked

through me, toss it out. Underneath all the layers
    of water I find Tío's mouth, it tells me:

I'm not going to hurt you. Then, his *shhh* floods me.
        In the morning, water leaks into my pillows.

Notes on Sueñitos

There are nights I catch lightning with my mouth. In dreams,
I disappear when Spanish comes out of me. I was told
I talk in my sleep. Even when asleep, my tongue can't decide
what I should be split into.
                    How heavy do you sleep,
my therapists asks. I tell her enough to dream of my parents
dying in Spanish, but when I open my mouth to yell their
names, it catches on fire.
                    Sueñitos, Amá called them that
when I was little. Sueñitos are not as pleasant as the word sounds.
Sometimes I ask Siri: What can I do to stop disappearing in Spanish?
Searching: I don't have an answer for that. Here's a definition for Spanish:
look in the mirror & go back to Mexico,
                    to México,
                    to Méjico,
                    a soñar.
In San Luis Potosí, my family says Tex-Mex Spanish isn't Spanish.
They tease me with *gringo*, *güero*, or *conquistador*. I let them soak
into my dreams. I conjure myself walking up the steps of the
pirámide del sol. Lightning has struck my tongue off. On a gold
platter, I carry it & I hand it over to my
                                        ancestors.

Amá Sees Fireflies

She stands outside, watches
  the roof of the house incinerate
    like newspaper caught on fire.

Copper chloride flares flash,
  bloom into a blaze. I watch
    behind her, the red shimmers remind me

of Abuelo. How he lit a cigarette,
  how flames touched the tip, how he
    inhaled smoke, let out fire. *Isn't it beautiful?*

she says. The firestorm brews &
  she laughs at sounds of sirens.
    The roof of our house collapses,

sparks flutter into the air.
  She laughs harder, speckles
    of ash fall on us. She twirls,

spirals of fire. People watch her—
  Amá the firework show.
    She keeps on repeating, *Ya soy libre.*

Ya soy libre. Ya soy libre, Papá—libre.
  She turns, grabs my hands, tells me: *Dance*
    with me. We spin in circles, our burning

house blurs into a field of hibiscus flowers.
      Amá lets go of my hands. I catch my balance.
          Flakes of debris come down. She tells me to

make a wish on one of the fireflies.
      I close my eyes, Amá sings the song she
          played in the house the day her father died:

Y volver volver, volver a tus brazos
      otra vez. The smell of soot &
          sway of fumes remind me of him—

Calamine

Iván sighs as he presses his fingernails against his skin
to find relief, but even in comfort scars can form.
    Blisters erupt from the pigment of his skin &
turn into scabs. Liquid oozes, drips. I see them
    falling from his face as he shoves his head against the pillow.

He has a plague he cannot overlook.
    It spreads like a children's contagious virus;
but this one kills. I lay in bed next to him. I watch
    his chest rise again & again. Then, I count his
blood-orange blemishes to fall asleep.
    I hear Amá's voice, *Dale tiempo.*

I remember once coming home from school
    covered in rashes. Amá knew what it was, la viruela.
I told her kids said I looked as if leeches sucked my blood
    or as if my sores were about to burst,
giving birth to a fleet of mosquitos.

    At night, I bathe Iván like my mother bathed me—
in a tube full of oats. I let lukewarm water ease his body
    to find salvation. Sitting in the tub, I pour water on him,
his rock head breaks the water & I watch
    oats slither down his body. Water makes him glow;
if only baths could cure diseases. I can hear the doctor's voice:
    Time kills.

After the bath, he says he's tired
    from having all this air inside his body
& it not being able to life him. I tell him to stand,
    grab a towel, scoop him, & carry him to our room.
I twirl us & he laughs. I say, *Houston! We have a problem,*
    Helicopter Iván is about to go down, requesting a safe landing,
Roger? I keep spinning, his laughter consumes
    his body & mine. He blurts out, *Permission to lay me down—*

over. Just like the summer fading against the cerros in El Paso
    on a late September evening, I lather my mosquito-bitten body
in a blush, the smell of itching reminds me
    of Amá sitting me on her bed telling me
I am a night sky covered in red stars.

That's when I remember him
    sitting on our bed with a smile,
my fingertips blooming with small
    dots of pink relief from touching his skin.
There—he sits in my head
    slathered in ointment.

13 Reasons Why Apá Fears Water

1.

Apá's body floats on weekend mornings. His
belly rises with each breath, one hand extends
next to his face, the other hangs on the side of
the bed.

2.

    Apá dreams of drowning: his body
immersed in dark waters, his hands grasp for
dryness. At dawn, he floods his room with his
brother's name. His voice breaks in mid-sleep.
I can hear his body fighting for air.

3.

        Apá works
his fifth night shift this week. He reaches back to
the floor wax machine, leans his chest on the handles,
& flips the ON switch. He watches the sponge
rotate as a stream flows out.

4.

        Apá chugs beer,
throws it back like water. I ask him if he wants
another, he nods. He cracks it open, brings it to
his lips, & downs the liquid. He crushes the can
with one hand & belches out all the air inside of
him.

5.

Apá's arms push against the current of
the Rio Grande, legs tread water. He searches
the surface for his brother. Apá listens to the
shift of the waves, they tell him what his next
move should be. Water crashes into his face; a
current takes him under, too.

6.

He scratches his
head, looks away from my eyes; I know he
doesn't want to see me fight against water when
I ask him to go to my swim meet. *It's okay*, I
tell him, *you don't have to come.* He smiles &
says, *I'm tired today, but I'll go next time.*

7.

He
takes us to the beach, watches our bodies break
tides. The waves crash into us & the ocean's
hands drag my brother into its mouth. Apá's
eyes follow my brother from the shore. He bites
his lip, sinks his feet deeper into the sand, shouts:
¡Carlos!

8.

A geyser of hot water shoots from the car
radiator. Apá burns his hand. He curses into the
air: *¡Pinche agua, hija de su puta madre!*

9.

At a drive-
thru car wash, water leaks in through the window.
Apá takes a napkin from the dashboard, but water
softens it apart. He looks around the car, nothing

can prevent water from coming in. As the sponge
roller presses on the windshield, he closes his eyes
& sighs.

10.

Water falls from the sky, Apá drives us
through a storm, I hold on to the arm rest. Rain beats
on the windshield, wipers whoosh water away. Apá
smirks, lowers my window. I flinch at the touch of the
cold wetness. He says, *It's just water.*

11.

Every March 31,
Apá takes white roses to the San Antonio River. He
drops all fourteen, the age of his brother, Carlos, who
drowned at the Rio Grande. He watches each flower
bob up & down as the calm current takes them south.
Their bodies don't drown.

12.

We watch Amá water
the plants outside, the summer breeze carries the smell
of wet dirt. Apá stares out into the distance. Amá
wets him with the hose, his eyes widen, his breathing
locks, but he laughs it off.

13.

After Apá's heart attack,
the doctor sends him to water therapy. Apá refuses:
Water doesn't heal everything. I convince him to go by
joining him. In the pool, his body struggles to move. I
tell him to walk toward me; he says he can't. I swim to
him, I ask him if he trusts me, he nods his head, & I
lean his body slowly onto the water. As he lets go of his
body, his feet rise up to the surface.

At Night My Body Waits

It's winter outside, sharp
    tree branches scratch
my window. I hear
    the sound of a train
passing. Tío slips
    into my bed, wraps his
hands around my boy body.
    Tightly, he cups my moon face,
whispers, *I'm not going to hurt you.*

    I lie in bed, think of my
brother & cousins: do you
    keep his secret too?

My voice underneath blankets
    grows smaller as his hands feed
off my body. At night, I wake up
    to a train in the distance.

At dinner, I see my Tío
    in the man sitting next to me,
his body demanding more space,
    his arm sitting on my leg
adding more weight than
    what I already carry.

The man at dinner
    tells me to smile more.

In those words, I remember
        Tío & I want to yell,
Rot in hell, motherfucker!
        but the man is not him.
After dinner, I play back
        the encounter. I ask myself if what
was underneath my clothes lured
        him, like it tempted my Tío to
touch me beneath blankets.
        Maybe that's why I sleep naked at
night, waiting for my Tío to show up
        in my bed, telling me to quiet down as
he puts the hand he'd high-fived me with
        over my mouth.

When I first came out, Amá asked
        if my Tío touched me.
I looked her in the eyes, shook
        my head, & I swallowed my Tío
whole again.

Tonight, winter comes gently &
        in the distance the sound of trains.
I lie naked in bed. My own hands
        yearning to touch my body
all the way.

Choo-choo

The day Amá stopped driving, her curls became undone,
her red manicure turned pastel pink, her throat lost the sound left in it—

when a car slammed into her, pushing it toward train tracks.
The wheels of her white Oldsmobile clenched to tracks the way a jaw latches

on to a bite. Amá's hands on the steering wheel, her foot still on the gas going nowhere,
my brother in the back of the car, his mouth opens: *Choo-choo—*

How in the distance a train was approaching.
Amá four months pregnant with me,

her fingers slip like water every time she presses the buckle.
My brother now yelling, *Choo-choo!*

I ask my therapist if trauma is a way of cheating death.
    Trauma is a way of reminding the body you're a survivor.

        A man pulls over, yanks open the back door. Grabs my brother's arm
            & pulls him out the car seat. He sets him down, *Don't move.*

            The man opens Amá's car door, *Señora, si no se baja*
                ahorita Usted va a dejar huérfano a su hijo.

      Amá lets go of the steering wheel, gets out of the car, runs to my brother.
            My brother laughs out, *Choo-choo!*

& tugs on Amá's shirt.
White pieces of metal scatter in the air like doves.

My therapist says, *Trauma can affect the body in many ways.*
It has a way of staying inside you the way music gets put on a vinyl,

a needle encrypting a melody in it forever.

Defying the Dangers of Being

At eight in the morning, on a Sunday, I run
through Scenic Drive in El Paso listening to Defying Gravity. I look down
at two countries meshing in the daybreak,
light beams & shadows wrestle between the border.

The wall will always be there, & I close my eyes,
I see my sixth-grade middle school counselor say:
Do you want to work with your hands indoors or outdoors?
I make a fist underneath the table, how easy it is for him

to say those words. He's fired a year later
for shouting at a student who wants to be more.

In Michigan, children are chanting, *Build the Wall, Build the Wall,*
Build the Wall, during lunch; they clench their hands,
& bang on tables. Threats too can echo at the speed of
sound. At 20 years old, Apá tried to quit his job at a
Mexican restaurant, his boss yelling at him:
Don't walk away from the cooking line
or I'll tell La Migra where you live.

21

Frightened of losing our chances of growing up in an American school system
Apá stays slamming trays on the cooking line for two more years.
My parents have lived more than half of their lives afraid.
　In 2009, they contributed to the 1.68 million undocumented
　　immigrants living in Texas; such a crime to be *living*.

　When people run Scenic every Sunday, do they
look down too & think how fucked-up it is to have division?
A biracial boy in New Hampshire is almost lynched.
　His mother posts pictures: the skin on his neck splitting
　open; his own flesh fighting against what others think it should be.
　　The children who did this to him are "children being children."

　　　My best friend's mom tells me when she was young
　　　the teacher washed her mouth with soap
　　　when Spanish came out of her.
　　　Micro bubbles forming on her tongue
cleansing it of such dangers.

I keep running looking down at the border, separating us from them.
I woke this morning to a text message from a friend:
　　　　Did you make it home safe?

　　　When Trump became president, I walked
　　　through campus the next day, the American flag
　　　upside down lining the path to the library,

stars & stripes in distress proclaiming: this is our America
now, our world shifting toward a different direction. Later I
go to dinner at L&J Cafe, watch two army men tell my waiter to go back
to México if he can't speak English right. I realize
this isn't *our* America, but *their* America.

The waiter's hand shakes as he gives me
my change, looks me in the eyes, tells me:
Be safe. Amá tells me every time I go to Cuidad Juárez
not to trust anyone. She's afraid one day I'll disappear in her country
like the way she has disappeared in my country for 27 years. In Juárez, I walk
Avenida 16 de septiembre with headphones on hoping no one sees my hips move
to the beat & take me for weak; when I come out at 21 to my parents
Amá said, *Please don't dress like them.*

In 2016, 49 of *them* die at a gay club,
Pulse, in Orlando, Florida. A man opened fire.
Policemen had to tune out ringtones coming from dead bodies
on the dance floor as they searched for survivors;
in an audio clip, the lullaby of ringtones is painful to hear.
Amá calls me in the morning, tells me she loves me.
Love is a state of being too:
a man cries for an hour in my car
after I pick him up from a car wreck.
I hold him in my arms,

he says I deserve someone who will love me the way
I love him. I want to kiss him, tell him love isn't measured.
I squeeze his hand instead, afraid of the thought of anyone looking at us
from the outside of my car.
Once at the Tacoma Airport, while waiting in the security line
I saw a family of four: a husband, wife, & two daughters,
the wife & one of the daughters being escorted away by officials.
The husband & the other daughter unable to touch them.
As the woman turned back to look at the man, she says words in
another language. I don't understand the syllables, only
the wailing echo in my ear, reminding me of him—

I cross the security line, vomit in the nearest restroom.
Did that man & I look like the family clenching on to
their loved ones in the form of sounds?
These days I'm scared of driving, fearing I'll faint,
cause a car wreck & die alone.
Alone is more home to me these days.

Last December, I celebrated New Year's in Puerto Rico.
Tía calls me to say if I keep this up I will
end up alone. I laugh,
tell her, *Who am I waiting for?*
She confuses alone for lonely. Words
can be a state of being, too. The weight of the words
Can you take me home

being whispered to me
on my 25th birthday by the man I love,
knowing the night would come to this as his partner
& two dogs wait for him at home. He holds my hand,
tells me he's sorry over & over.
All I hear is the wind hitting
my window as I speed.

Every Sunday I come down from Scenic
Drive, I sing at the top of my lungs:
I'm defying gravity!
& you won't bring me down,
bring me down, bring me—
                    down!
            I smile knowing I burned my tongue
this morning drinking tea, thank God
for living another day,
oversee my two countries coming down
in front of my eyes
from Scenic Drive.

Second Wave

The Boy y El Hombre Que se Comió El Relámpago

The sky of Salitrillos, México, flickered down on
        Abuelo, young, driving his faded F-150
     on unpaved roads, the sky groaning,
     coughing lightning. He sped,
   not wanting to be caught in the storm, his
  whole body bobbed when he ran over rocks on the
road. Abuelo was too busy

        holding the steering wheel to notice the sky burst
      into shards of glass, a ball of
    fire bouncing in his lap. When he saw it he yelled,
   ` *Chinga su madre*, tried to blow it out like candles
on a birthday cake, but it seemed to grow, laugh.

    He pulled over, opened the door to throw it out,
   yet the sphere felt like he was
  touching life for the first time. As he
gasped in disbelief, the ball of fire went inside

      of him. Abuelo was found a day later by his
     compadre passed out inside his troca. He went
   down in his pueblo as el hombre que se comió
  el relámpago.

The day I drove from El Paso to San Antonio
for winter break I got caught in a storm too.
When the sky cracked down, my windshield blurred,
I pulled over. I remembered Abuelo's story,
asked myself if we inherit our ancestors' experiences,
if I have lightning inside of me.

When Amá's heart was struck by lightning
I remember she called Apá's name.
We found her in the kitchen, her whole body
bending & twisting, Apá holding her head,
Aquí estoy, aquí estoy. Amá couldn't
hear him, she kept twitching. When the ambulance
arrived, she was conscious, but she didn't remember

what happened to her. After the stroke
Amá became a storm, her rage would last minutes
then as if nothing had happened. For years I have
wondered what broke inside her.

When my ex-boyfriend & I had late-night talks in the
back of my GMC Sierra, we would tell each other
stories of ourselves. I told him about Abuelo.
He laughed so hard that night he said, *You're full
of shit.* I shrugged my shoulders, then told him, *How
else do you think we make sparks when we kiss?*

He said, *Tell me something you've never told anyone before.*
I stayed quiet for a bit, then said, I wish I was light, to be
translucent, to be able to pass through someone's body.
He got on top of me that night, unzipped
my pants, leaned down to kiss me. *You don't
have to be light to pass through someone's body.*

The day Abuelo died, he was sitting outside smoking
his last cigarette, his hair damp from his shower,
his right leg crossed on his left leg, his shirt unbuttoned
halfway, so he could feel the night breeze, a Coca-Cola
glass bottle on the side of the chair. As he got up, his right
arm twisted, fingers curled, his mouth clenched, his eyes

almost burst. He shouted for my Abuela, she called
for my Tíos, their feet picked up dirt & debris as they
all carried Abuelo's body into the back of the F-150
pickup truck. They said his body looked like a relámpago
zigzagging uncontrollably.

Then Abuelo took one last breath,
all at once his whole body releasing
the electricity inside him.

When the storm passed, I looked up at the sky, thought of
how many things pass through clouds, of how it will be when
lightning comes out of me, will my body curve, braid itself into all my
ancestors & surrender to the sky?

Dear Iván

I forgot you yesterday so

    I sped to the cemetery to say, *I'm sorry.*

        I didn't sleep last night again in fear of forgetting your dimples.

My therapist asks me, *How are you dealing?*

    Fine.

        The truth is I'm not eating

again. I only chew the syllables of your name

    at 2:45 a.m.,

        the time of your death.

People say depression looks good on me

    as in to say I look fine.

        I once met a man in South Korea, he was *fiiiiiiine.*

Snowflakes gathered on his eyelashes

    when we walked through Seoul.

        He sort of sounded like you when I was inside him.

I thought I saw you at the gas station a week after your death.

He had your face, I swear. Iván,

didn't you say you wouldn't die on me?

At night, when it's dark in my room I Google: *Are the dead fine?*

I can hear your brother's voice say, *He's gone.*

Sometimes I get so high, I think about not coming down.

Then, I think of the last joint we smoked together at 22:

How you bloated, belly big in smoke & exhaling,

how the whole room filled with clouds & laughter,

how you turned to look at me & said, *Get up & fly high.*

Your brother texted me last week,

How are you doing?

I said, *I'm fine.*

I didn't have the heart to tell him

to stop texting me.

My therapist says, *People look for comfort in others*

because love is a way of haunting.

I look for comfort in other men who can hold me like

you did. A man once asked me to kiss him with my eyes

open. *My ex-boyfriend used to kiss me like this.*

It's been eight years now

& every time I wear your T-shirt to sleep

I dream in the only tongue I know I'll find you in—

in the language of grief.

That's Not My Name

In the fifth grade, I wanted to tuck my name
beneath my teacher's tongue. I thawed
on mornings, prepared myself as she went down the
roster, ashamed to ask her to not yawn my name

around. The classroom eyes *ahh*, & I hunch a little;
they know she's merging two syllables into
one. My ears felt the snap of her jaw as she opened
her mouth all day calling my name.

                                   With each jab
my back got heavy, hauling the weight of two
languages. Once, on a field trip, a woman

pressed a permanent marker against a name
tag, her blue eyes tracing every letter. She called me
Sal. I wanted to stand tall but translucent
I became. I heard many names that afternoon, from

my teacher, strangers, friends. Toward
the end, they didn't know what to
call me. *The Spanish kid* made its way mouth-to-
ear-to-mouth; a child can only take so much taunting.

How to tell them my name has soul: I should have
said how my name in Spanish stays in your
tongue, a little longer; how I am the unyielding color
azul. I know now not all tongues move, fold,

press against teeth to reach for
more. The tongues I now know
I can bend; I can say to people
That's not how you say my name.

On the school bus, I sat alone in the back,
pressed my mouth against the window,
& breathed against it. In the mist, I wrote
my name & watched it

vanish, again—
again
again
again
again

& again

When a Body Is Dragged

For four miles Emmanuel is caught

    underneath a car. Across streets & railroad tracks,

his body peels away. Each time the gas pedal is stepped on

    his body untangles, leaves chunks

of skin behind. Witnesses say they could hear him screech

    for help. Witnesses say they didn't know

where the echoes were coming from—because the car

    was too low, because it was nighttime, because we freeze

in moments of terror. The car in motion was going the speed limit,

    35 mph. The driver had a blood alcohol concentration over .08.

I wonder if Emmanuel was aware, if he was

    witnessing his own death. I'm reminded of a woman

who yelled, *HELP ME* as a man pushed her head to the cement in front

    of our house, taking her in a black 1980s Camaro. I was ten. Amá clenched my body close to hers. The black Camaro drove fast; we could hear

her scalp crack. Fear is stronger than bravery in moments of terror.

We learned in the news of the woman & her captures. How the cops found scraps of
her scalp against the asphalt.

When the police stopped the car with Emmanuel's body underneath it, the
firefighters took an hour to undo his body

from below the car. His body still breathing. They laid him

on a stretcher, rushed him to the ER. In the morning the headlines of
Wednesday's newspaper say: *Texas man dies in hospital after car drags him 4 miles.*

The news doesn't say, when the cops laid him on the stretcher & rushed him to the ER,

he was still breathing. Which meant he held on until he was embraced—

this too is survival.

Tessellation

The day lightning came out of Amá, she was in the kitchen,
her hands full of foam from dish soap, her hair undone,
she wore jeans, a black T-shirt with an apron Abuela sent her
from México. Her shriek for help is what haunts me the most.
The way her mouth in one last action of survival spelled out Apá's name:
AR-RRRR-TUUU-RR-OOO.

Scientists say we recognize sound even before we are born.
At night, the sound of Amá's body collapsing ripples.
I wake up thinking how Amá can be at many places at once
without leaving her body. The ringing of her voice vibrates
into my ear, reminds me she's still here. In my sleep, I hear her:
AR-RRRR-TUUU-RR-OOO.

Amá's tongue curled up, snail-like; for three months it had
to be straightened out again. The doctor stated: *This is
common after a stroke, shocks travel throughout the body.
Sometimes a person has to learn the basics.* For three months,
I watched over Amá's body, how her mouth repositioned & called for
AR-RRRR-TUUU-RR-OOO.

For three months, I saw Amá's right side begin to shift
back into place. Her curved fingers unlocking from the tension,
the cracking of her bones moving to a familiar place.   Twelve years
later & her body is still relocating.   Twelve years later & I
can still hear her voice tessellate in & out of my body:

AR-RRRR-TUUU-RR-OOO

La Doppelgänger

In the bright light of the kitchen table,
I watch Amá take a thin blade. Cuts out

numbers from a card, transfers them to
another. She takes a magnifying glass,

holds it from a distance to not give the
words & numbers she's putting together

heat. She looks at me, *Quítate con tu coca.*
I watch her create a new identification from across

the room. Years later, I'll visit a man at 17
& ask him to create a new identity for me the way

Amá did that night. I'll watch him cut
& shape a new me, not to survive, but to drink.

After Amá put herself into a new identification card,
she shows me & says, *Dale gracias a Dios que tú nunca tendrás*

que hacer esto. In the morning, we mourn the death
of a citizen & welcome the life of a doppelgänger.

Amá lights a candle to St. Judas & asks me to pray
to the universe with her, so doors can open for her.

I kneel next to her, hoping this plastic card can give her
the status she most desires. I didn't know at the time

sometimes to survive you have to transform—

Amá, you once told me: Hay cosas de las que no puedes saber—& there are secrets about me you cannot know too. The way in which you do not want to talk about your past, our past, isn't healing anyone of us. When you hit me for having a limp wrist, I should've known it was Tatarabuela coming out of you telling you: *You have*

to teach your children how to   *survive.* Survival, what our family
has always done. The way   you've told me you'd eat
nothing but tomatoes &   beans to live & why you
served us bones in   broth to give the water
flavor. When my   brother graduated high
school you cried. I   didn't know it meant
we've all survived.   The first man I kissed
was in a hotel room.   I was 20, I wanted to
know if what I felt   inside would let me live
& it did—maybe that's   why we can't say
I love you when we hang   up the phone. When my
Great-Tío convinced   Tatarabuelo to announce in a

What Is a Cycle if Not a Circle

town meeting only he would inherit all of his money & land, none of us knew it was the beginning of survival for generations to come. Tatarabuelo didn't know his dementia would affect our history. I've been scared of erasure, of waking up one day & not recognizing myself. What if survival is a lifetime? Amá, can you tell me what you keep under your tongue? I need to know how to turn a circle into a
line.

For My Queer Ancestors

Somewhere across the border,
beyond the desert,
beyond cerros,

my family history
is erased each day.
But I only know them by name:

> Federico

> Elvira

> Antonio

> Magdalena

Maybe you, too, held
hands with a boy like you
or a girl like you?

> Matheo

> Griselda

> Luis

> Zoraida

To take a leap,
means sometimes losing your family:

Gustavo

Micaela

Ángel

Esmeralda

If I lose them I will ask
you to help me find myself,

Arnulfo

Esperanza

Luis Mario

Marisol

If you can read this,
I'm losing myself.

Alfonzo

Mariela

Jacundo

Carmen

In México, I ask
Abuelo if anyone in
our family is gay,

he says, *En nuestra sangre
there aren't any of them,*

& I say:

                    Tomás

                    Francis

                    ⎯⎯⎯

                    ⎯⎯⎯

But he walks away.

Third Wave

The Boy & The Story of Water

I

There are stories about boys like me who become water
                in a bathtub. Sound underwater doesn't travel.

II

        Two truths & a lie:
(1) The Aztec deity of water, Chalchiuhtlicue, released fifty-two years of rain,
           drowned the fourth sun, created Earth, turned people into fish;
               (2) Water has memory;
            (3) Learning to swim will not help you save a life.

III

        Apá drives my brother & I to Corpus Christi,
        Lo más importante no es saber nadar   si no como flotar para que no te ahoges.
At the beach, my brother is tall enough to stand
             in the water. Afraid of the current, I grab on to Apá's waist, but
          Apá throws me in. I land near the bottom of the ocean, my body starfish like.
He pulls me up from the sand,
          Qué te pasa, debes dejar ir el aire en tu cuerpo.

IV

            Once upon a time in México, Apá & his brother stuffed their lives
into a knockoff JanSport backpack: birth certificates,
           identifications, pictures, a rosario, one pair of clean clothes,
& a water bottle. Their last night in México, they bended their hands like waves,
           asked God for a safe crossing into America.
They slept on the benches of the church. In the morning, they set off
           on a four-day journey up north toward Texas. They forgot to

calculate how fast water evaporates, the strength of the Rio Grande
running to the Gulf, how water swims on your skin,
consumes your body. The river folded & folded & folded his brother's body under its
thickness.
Apá learned not all rivers are meant to be crossed.

V

At the Gulf of México, Apá dips his feet in & out of the water, I
wonder if he feels close to México, to his brother. If part of Chalchiuhtlicue's
vengeance is to
turn men into fish, is my Tío out there?

VI

At the beach, a wave takes my brother in,
Apá sinks his feet into the sand, calls out to my brother.
A white man yanks my brother out.
Apá tells my brother, *Crees que sabes el camino de la agua, eh?*
The white man tells Apá, *Why didn't you do something?*   Apá freezes, *¿Qué dijo?*
—I tell him what the white man said, Apá buries his feet deeper into the
sand, looks down. *I thought all wetbacks knew how to swim,*
the white man laughs, turns to his friends, points at Apá, *Look—*
a wetback   who doesn't know   how to swim.

VII

I have dreams of diving into a pool,
when I pick up my head I'm on the surface of the Gulf of México,
I pull against currents, I hear the man calling Apá *wetback,*
the closer I get to them the farther the waves push me. I go under.
Water goes inside of me
until I know the weight of it. I reach the bottom
of the ocean where I call for my Tío
until I become sea foam.

Meditation on Grief

My therapist says, *Grief is like filling a balloon with water*
    until it gets so heavy it bursts. I think of Apá,

how when he arrived to the States, he drank so much beer
    you could smell his brother's suffocation on him; how he still sits outside,

searches the night sky for his brother's face. He was never taught to mourn.
    Instead, he carries grief inside like me. When it rains, he takes cover so he

won't fill up & burst like my Tía. When she lost her husband, we would carry
    her like water in our arms, lay her in the tub, run cold rivers all over her body

until it would enter her skin like knives—& she'd yell: MARIO! My therapist says,
    Grief comes at different stages in our lives. I tell her somedays I wake up

to Amá's voice ringing in my ear, *I can't go to México,* how Amá sent me
    to bury her father when she couldn't go, how my brother & I carried

my Abuelo's casket around the town, our bodies on the verge of collapsing from all
the weight.
    My therapist asks, *How does that make you feel?* I tell her it reminds me of a
recurring

dream: Apá & I stuck in a flash flood while driving.
    She says, *Grief can manifest in dreams.* In mine, water leaks through

the thin cracks of our car door, Apá looks at me, *No tengas miedo.*
    The doors won't open, neither of us can break the windshield, & we laugh until

water goes inside of us.

Notes on Dividing Fractions

My math teacher points to my test grade marked in red, & I hate looking at
  numbers; they remind me of distance & loss. *Pull it together*, he says.

After school, he tells me, *I get it; numbers & stuff like that scare you.* I put my head
down, use my nails to chip away at the grade marked in red. He pats my back & says:
Let's look at division & then we'll move into fractions. I'll need you to look up, though.

He has no idea my immigrant parents have been divided so many times in this
country, their memories an unsolved math problem.

He has no idea a fraction to me means leaving traces of my culture behind, or
how embarrassing it is to say—*My parents are from México*, as in my parents are
undocumented, as if to say they came here to give me a country that wants me dead.

How do I tell him math for me means watching my parents multiply dollar
bills to purchase calling cards from the corner store to make calls to México. Every
time they call, the division problem grows. There is no reciprocal for the border. The
boarder is a factor to this math problem.

Pushing My Name Down Their Bodies

After "Pulling the Moon" by Marcelo Hernandez Castillo

I've made love to many men.
I've made love to many men but they don't know my name.

       I push their bodies out of the moon.

Out of the moon I push their bodies & eat them again.

       I line them up, push each of their torsos
to my lips, plead with them to remember the syllables of my name.
Each man turns me around, grabs the inside of my thighs,
pull my hips toward them. Their hands create craters on my body.

When I throat them, they say, *Your parents
made you out of love.*

At night I ask the moon, *Tell me what you know
                about love.*

The moon goes back & forth,
    pulls the sweat out of my thighs
    where the next man,
       & the next,
     & the next, will put his lips
on & say, *Dammn, baby, can I fuck you?*

I spit my name into all the mouths of the men
who have fucked me.

But they all leave before morning, before knowing it.
Their tongues ready to go down on the next man.

I'll close the door behind me,
pull all the men out of me, ask,
Why don't you love me?

MISSING TÍO

Please,   have you seen him

    crossing the Rio
      Grande

He's wearing a face

    I only see in

dreams

    Please

    do you have info

        Please, help him

He cannot swim

    Please

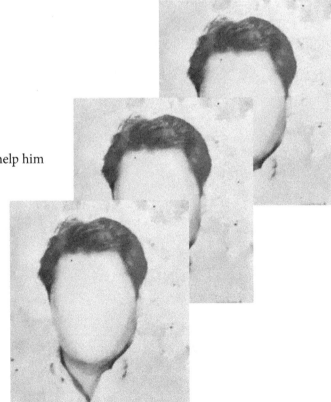

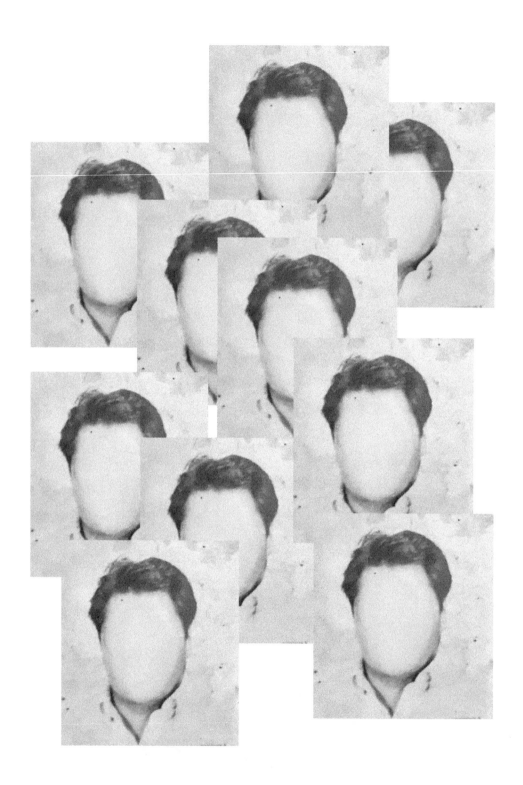

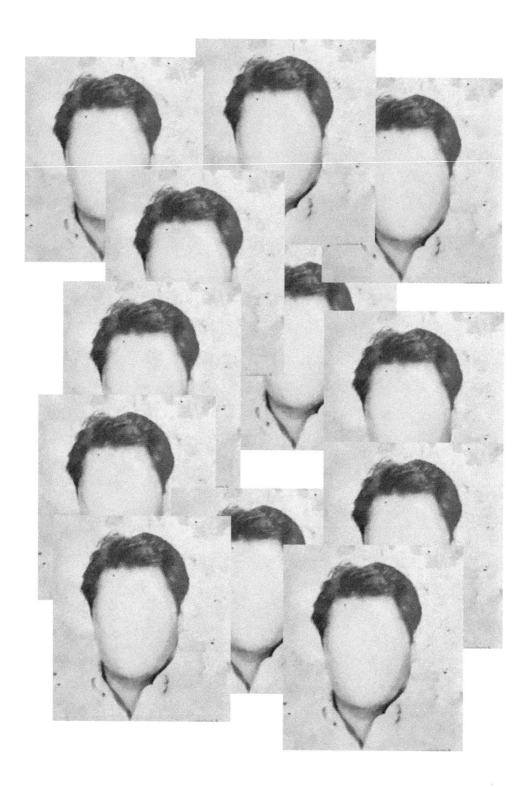

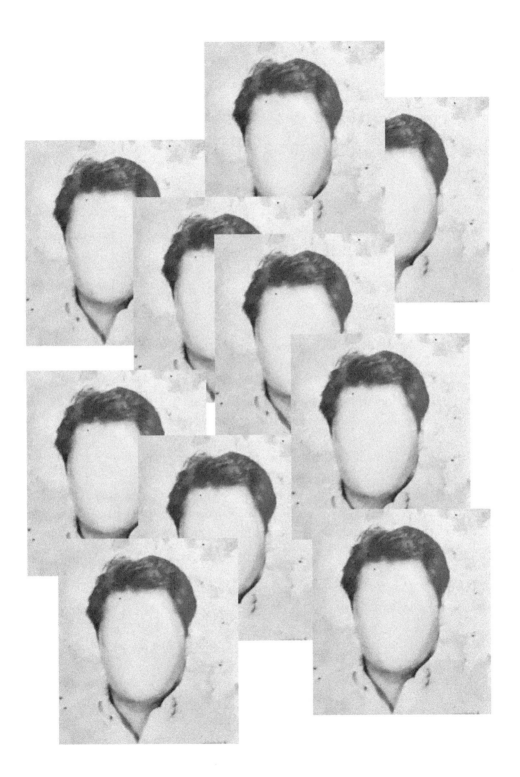

How to Outline a Body: Fragments after Tatarabuela Ignacia's Passing

1. My Tías say when Abuela Ignacia's essence left her body, you could hear one long sigh stretch from her insides to every corner of the room.

2. We made a fire outside. We all talked about what to do with her body.

3. The first time I went to México, I was 12. I remember seeing her in the kitchen making tortillas from scratch. The smell of masa in the air, I could hear her hands pounding, see her long braid reaching past her waist, it moving side to side.

4. Half of her children wanted to burn her: *Esa no es mamá, es nada más que un cuerpo.* The other half wanted to bury her because a body needs rest.

5. The fire lasted all night while they argued back & forth.

6. Abuela asked me what I wanted to eat on my first night in México. *Un pollo.* 30 minutes later, I walked in on her severing a chicken by the neck, like the way grief circles around you. Then, she set it on the table & began to peel off the feathers with her fingers.

7. The doctor came in the morning, injected Abuela's body with a decomposing vaccine. He said, *Para que no huela el cuerpo.*

8. At the time, I didn't know a body rots from the inside by first releasing gases. Even after death, a smell can follow you.

9. In her room, I found pictures of her under her bed inside a Ziploc bag. Abuela's smiling holding Abuelo's arm. When I opened the bag, tortillas filled the room.

10. I watched my tías wash her body with a sponge. They raised her arms up, gently scrubbed every crevice of Abuela's body.

11. Two of my tías brushed her white hair out & braided it. They mentioned how her hair used to be red, like the fire still burning outside.

12. At the viewing todo el pueblo came. Over 500 people came to pay their respects.

13. I wondered, how does a body receive so much love even after death?

14. At the viewing, I went up to her casket & with my index finger I outlined her body. I made sure to remember the round shape of her nose, how her hair felt like soft lace.

15. Abuela was always moving: cleaning, cooking, taking care of others, feeding animals. It was strange to see her so still.

16. When we buried Abuela the next day I thought about her last breath, if part of her soul came out with it, if she's watching us from the trees.

17. The night Abuela died, she came to me in a dream. She opened my mouth with her thin fingers, then she exhaled all her breath into me. Inside of me, a fire ignited. She tied my mouth with strands of her hair. Then she said: *Tienes que sobrevivr.*

18. One of my tías said she saw Abuela in the kitchen making coffee.

19. I hung up my favorite picture of her. Abuela's young, sitting outside on the street. Her legs are crossed, her back arching forward as if trying to reach you. Her fiery hair in a braid. Her left arm's resting on her knee & her right hand is in the air, holding a bitten prickly pear. Her mouth's half open, as if to say: *Acuérdate lo que te dije.*

Water Runs Too

The portrait of desperation was captured on Monday by the journalist Julia Le Duc, in the hours after Óscar Alberto Martínez Ramírez died with his 23-month-old daughter, Valeria, as they tried to cross from Mexico to the United States.

—*New York Times*, 2019

It's June, rain falls all day in Austin,
          water rushes down gutters,
down stems of plants, down the sidewalk.
     Down my throat a photograph surfaces:
two bodies belly flat on the banks
     of the Rio Grande. News anchors tug each other,
raising the bodies toward an audience,
     their mouths tread water when they speak.

At the gym, the image displays on four different TVs.
     No one looks up. On the stair master I go up another level, let my legs go numb.
The news says, *The current took them*—
     the word *illegal* breaks through each screen & overflows the night.

When the river splits open its mouth,
     will people raise questions instead of bodies?
At night, I lie awake, think about what's beneath the river.
       Will we find our fathers,
          our mothers,
             our sisters,
          our brothers,
             our cousins,
             my Tío—

Ars Poética for a First G(ay)eneration Mexican American

I lick every drop of sperm off a white man's navel,
    put my lips on his shaft,
his hand grips the back of my neck.
    I open my mouth to swallow again,
Tell me something in Spanish.
    Sound of my slob in the air,
Tell me something
        in Spanish, Tell me
something in Spanish,
        tell me something
          in Spanish.
    That's how English asphyxiates me.

    When the doctor pulled me out of Amá by my legs,
        my body came out in the shape of the letter *Y*.
    When the nurse asked Amá what she would name me
she took off the accent from my name.
    Gave me to English at birth. Sometimes I ask myself,
    Is Spanish my first language
  or is it shame?

In the third grade, my ESL teacher handed me English
    in a book. Every word entered me
the way I penetrated a white man: eager & willing.

Yesterday, I was reminded the word *animal*
      is spelled the same in English & Spanish;
when the white Border Patrol agent spilled water on the floor
      & told Apá, *Drink, you animal!*

I don't remember at what age I became a translator
      for my parents. My earliest memory is at the hospital,
telling the doctor the symptoms Amá was feeling.

      When I told my parents *I'm gay*
          I didn't need to translate.
      To ask for help has the same sound in any language.

More than once a white man has broken into me—
      a cop on night duty licked my neck, *I love Latin men.*
      Afterward, his head on my stomach,
Last night I arrested a man who looked like you.

      One morning I heard Amá practicing English
          from an Inglés Sin Barreras tape. She wrote down words
          on her notepad, mimicked the sound from the white man.
      English has a pulse, I could hear it in her throat

            & in mine.

The Rio Grande Speaks

Everyone claims to know my waters

I've been known as a force of nature

Sometimes I'm all muscle, no grace

Many have crossed me & I've crossed many

I answer to no one, not even to myself

Sometimes I'm all grace, no muscle

You've seen my body rough but never smooth

I do have memory & I do remember

They call me El Rio Grande,
El Rio Bravo, Big River, La Frontera

Everybody wants to give me a name

But no one wants to know me

For years, I've pulled bodies into the pit of my belly

& a body is always hungry

Truth is, I answer to no one, not even to myself—

I wish you could feel the weight of my body

I'm tired of having a body I can't control

Fourth Wave

The Boy & The Sound of Himself

I

I was ~~obsessively~~ jealous of parrots, how
they can mimic sound. Speak without

the weight words carry. Sometimes
I dream of digging my fingers into

the beak of a parrot, splitting it open.
Searching for all the sounds

it has ever heard. At the library,
I undo what's beneath my tongue,

whisper to the dictionary:

      Am I   Am I   Am I—

II

Not everything you do needs a word,
Amá says, drying my body with a
fresh towel. I can smell the sun on it
from it being on the clothesline all day.

She wraps me in a yellow cobertor.
Her mouth slides words into existence,
Te ves más mejor así.

In the living room, Apá throws back a beer while
gays fight for their rights on the news.
He takes a glimpse of me in yellow, squeezes the
beer can in his right hand, burps, spells out
with his yeast breath into the air:
Maricones pendejos.

I remove the blanket off me, drag it to my room.

The word
      maricón
            not far
                  behind me.

Everything I do needs a word.

III

In college, I read Gertrude Stein,
a rose is a rose is a rose—
I unravel petals all day
with my tongue. I tease a boy,
tell him I don't like anything
going in me, unless it's love.
We laugh.

In the morning I ask him,
What would you call
what we did last night?
His answer: *We don't*
have to call it anything.

& he's right.

Unless it's love   unless it's love   unless—

IV

As a child I once asked Amá:
Am I . . .

while wearing her blouse, covered in
a yellow & blue regurgitation of flowers.

She opened her mouth to slaughter me.

V

Sometimes in my dreams / I don't kill the parrot / it's free /
it flies high above / where there is no sound

just vibrations / waves of the wind
coming together / pushing into ears / never the mouth /

I wake up / find my mouth full of ellipsis /
I need sounds / for where I am living

This Is Why I Fall Fast

When I was a boy, I had jump   scare nightmares. I was always falling   into
unknown spaces. At nine years old, Amá took me to a curandera, *Señora, este niño se
me cae en la noche.* The curandera grabbed rose petals, dipped them into a bowl with
oil, took pieces of my hair, spit into the bowl, picked up a Cuban cigar, lit it with her
fingertips. She told Amá, *Mire, señora, yo puedo con todo.*   She puffed
smoke into the bowl, grabbed it with both hands, tossed everything into the sky.
When the oiled rose petals hit the floor, I collapsed.   The curandera rattled her
hands, whispered something into the spaces of the room,   said out loud:
Él ya no se va a caer en las noches.   For 10 years I never fell.   I didn't have
nightmares.   I was healed.   Then at 19, I kissed a man in a hotel room.
He said,

I can fall

for a guy like you

as he brushed his rough hands across my cheeks; he kissed them until his lips got
chapped. I told him, *No one has ever done that to me.*   *Did you like it?*
He kissed them all night until my toes curled. I fell asleep in his arms, woke up to the
sound of bed sheets shaking.   For three years,   I met up with men in hotel
rooms.   When they whispered into my body their moans   I fell hard &
fast for them. Hard & fast   Fast &   hard   Hard & fast Fast &
hard   Hard   & fast Fast & hard   Hard &   fast Fast   & hard Hard   & fast
Fast & hard Hard & fast   Fast & hard   Hard &   fast Fast &   hard Hard
&   fast Fast & hard Hard & fast Fast & hard   Hard & fast Fast   & hard
Hard &   fast Fast   & hard   Hard & fast   Fast &
hard   Hard   &   fast   I fell for a man who gave me cocaine.
One night

I asked him: *Why do you like men?*

Because they fall for me easy.

After a line or two, he was right.

The night before he overdosed, he told me:

Don't fall for men like me.   After his death, I went back to the curandera, *Señora, can you help me?*   She took out her Cuban cigar, lit it again with her fingertips,   inhaled   &   coughed out   white moths.

She said: *Mijo, this is what is inside of you.*   She caught a moth with her hand & handed it to me.   *No   puedes   volar*

si   sigues

callendo.

The Girl & The Northern Lights

When Amá was 12, she would lie under a blanket of stars in Salitrillos, San Luis Potosí,
MX, count every dream she had. The nights in Salitrillos thick
    as the lights in the cities she imagined up north. Some things are hard to see when
all you have around you are stories; people would come back to build houses, buy trucks,
buy land, they'd say, *En El Norte el dinero se da de donde quiera.* Amá would
ask, *Y cómo es allá,* pointing toward the North. The people would tell her,

    Muchacha, usa tu imaginación. Amá would close her eyes,
lights of El Norte tracing her body, an ocean of bright waves guiding her way down
    paved streets, houses like money, streets in American movies; there she
didn't have to think about money, all she had to do was stretch her hand
    into the air & money would appear. At sixteen she packed a suitcase, put
on blue jeans & a white button-up because that's how woman dressed in America,
    she told Salitrillos *¡Adiós!* as she held her permit in her left hand, an image card
of St. Judas in her right hand. In Laredo, TX,

    Amá thought she would see the Statue of Liberty
across the border welcoming her; instead she saw a gray sky.
    The first song she heard in English was played by her cousins, "Deep in The
Heart of Texas." When she asked them for the translation, they laughed,
    Las estrellas brillan aquí bien bonito en la noche. She waited at night in San

Antonio for las estrellas to appear; there were no stars, the pollution covered

the skies, but she didn't care, Amá was in America. For twenty-eight years, she lit

candles of St. Judas to show her the light.

When she received her green card, she held it up to the sky, light in her fingertips

radiating behind the sun. For the first time in twenty-eight years

Amá saw the northern lights accepting her into a country where she became a woman,

a mother, a grandmother, a dreamer. When I ask her,

Amá, what did you think of the States when you were a girl? she says, *Ya ni me*

acuerdo . . . Nada mas me recuerdo de muchas luces. A kaleidoscope of running lights

like water in a stream, everything blurry coming into chrysalis blinding the past.

The Loquat Trees & The Boy Next Door

His smile captured rays of sunlight
in between his teeth. The smell of
    summer around us. In my backyard
I met him, white tee, washed-out
    blue jeans. He plucked off a
loquat from a branch. Handed
    one to me. *Open your mouth*, he said.
    When I tried to speak, he shoved
his loquat-soaked fingers inside.
    For six years I ate them. The sweetness
& tart remind me of his finger,
    a whisk in my mouth. He once took out
a pocketknife. His finger slid against
    the blade. I asked him, *What do you
plan to do with that? What else but
    peel the fruit.* Afterward, his sticky fingers on my skin,
we lay that afternoon under
    the loquat trees, bellies full of sunshine.
When the loquat trees stopped giving fruit, I planted seeds.
    I waited next spring for him to meet me under the trees & peel the fruit.
Instead, gravity pulled down the fruits.
    I ate with a hunger I've never felt before.
No one told me hunger & heartache feel the same.

Airball

In Juárez, a boy clenches his hands
against the gate. He watches a show:
a group of boys playing basketball on the other side,
at Bowie High School. His eyes watch the ball
as it's dribbled & passed around. His eyes continue
to watch for an opening. The boy's hands grip
the fence tighter as another boy falls on the opposite side,
misses the shot. The boys laugh at him,
as he gets up from the floor, they all shake hands
& leave the court. The boy across the fence
in Juárez keeps watching the possibilities
of how the game could have ended:
a 3-pointer, a 2-pointer or
an access shot to
outweigh the odds.

How to Find the Distance between Two Points

Use the equation:
$$d = \sqrt{(\chi_2-\chi_1)^2 + (y_2-y_1)^2}$$

to solve for what my undocumented
Apá & Amá couldn't touch
for 28 years.

The points are:
San Antonio, TX, USA (29.42, 98.49)
San Luis Potosi, SLP, MX (22.15, 100.95)

Then, multiply the answer by ∞
to solve for the distance
they carry.

My Love Would Have Killed You

Listen / do you remember / the night I drove 95 on a 50 / gripping the steering wheel with one hand / with the other hand clenching your jaw / begging you to tell me you love me / *Say it like you mean it* / I told you that / while you shouted / *Look at the road* /
                                        the lights on the road fading
us by / you said / *If you love me you'll slow down* / I was afraid to press the brake too fast / love isn't about losing /

                                look / hear me out / after you / I've been trying to slow down / I met another / the way he laughs reminded me of you / but he doesn't know me like you / I called him your name once / he gazed into my eyes / searching for an answer / the way you would / I tried to laugh it off / my throat closing / he cupped my face / held it with both of his hands / with his soft voice / he said / *I know you're thinking about him* / *it's okay* / *one day you won't think of him* / *everything will pass by like lightning* / *memory is like that* / *& you'll only remember love*

Breath Is a Body at War

Before the body knows breath, it knows war.
     The way there was a war inside the hands of Abuelo,
who plucked tomatoes off vines until his hands were
         left purple & red. Who passed down his hands
to Apá & how his hands smelled of gasoline & oil, no matter
     how many times he washed. Who passed down his hands to me.

Outside a bar, a drunk man gives me a fireball kiss, heat goes
     inside of me. Afterward, he shoves his fist
         into my face. Calls me *faggot*.
This man wants to kill me because
     we breathe the same air.

War is like that, silent in movement—like my
     Abuela who collects paper towels everywhere she goes
         because they were a luxury for her growing up.
She used to stack them in her purse until her bag slipped off her shoulder,
     the wind blew out every napkin flying
& she jumped for every white piece like as if they were dollar bills.

     A war has edges, like the man at the gym who wears a "guns out" shirt.
Who later tells me: *Come to my house,*
     where he kneels on the floor in front of me,
         licks my fingers until he gags on them.
He lays on all fours, begs: *Put your fist inside me.*

There are truths I'll never know in this body.
When immigration called out Amá's name incorrectly,
    she corrected them, as if to say the border can take everything away
        but it can't take away my name.

Before Abuelo died, my tíos & Abuela said he fought his own body
to breathe. They said he made his hands into fists. I imagine him
    telling himself: *Todavía no es mi tiempo.*

A man once sat in my bed, his body buzzing. I told him:
We don't have to do anything if you don't want to.
    We sat in silence holding hands for an hour. When he turned to kiss me,
        he said: *Do you know God is watching us?*

For more than half of my life, I've asked my hands why they wanted to touch
a man. But even a war must have a home

        & like this poem before it knew it would even have a line—
        maybe it too clenched its hands & fought for breath.

.

Fifth Wave

The Boy & The Lineage of Dreams

My family has only ever had dreams.
    Before language, my ancestors saw visions
        of the future.

For centuries they questioned what moves faster:
    light or dreams.

        · *Where do you go when you fall asleep?*
        my ex-boyfriend used to ask me.

        Tonight, my dreams spill faster than water.

They end the same as every night:

In the middle of Abuelo's milpa in México,
    I find my body on top of other bodies.
        We all have one thing in common:
            love
                for other men.

Here, the dead echo:
    The past is never the past.

        & I keep asking them the same question:

        What's going to happen to a boy like me?

When Dreams Come True

I

The telephone rings at three
in the morning, the receiver shouts
into Amá's ear: *¡Papá está muerto!*

Her eyes widen, her fingers rattle
with the news, she drops the phone;
her llanto a waking lullaby—

some dreams do come true. She
paces the house running her fingers through
her hair. In the morning, a sixteen-hour drive to

México awaits. In the driveway, the truck is parked, ready
for her. The word *illegal* rolls out
of her siblings' mouths & they console

her choice. My Tío turns the key &
her body thrusts out of the back seat.
Amá stares at my brother & me

from outside of the SUV. She tells us to go
in her place. The truck pulls out of the driveway
toward the direction of the country

she left behind at 15. She stays
in the driveway, her hands stretch out
for what is impossible for her to

reach.

II

I play a video at night: families meet in
the middle of the Rio Grande with
their ankles in water, reuniting. In

180 seconds, they grab on to one another, dig
their faces in between necks, fingers that
do not want to let go of one another. A

couple drives 11 hours from a small town in México
to meet their grandchildren for the first time. A
woman says it's been a decade since she

has seen her family. A girl of 15 says
her mother was deported years ago;
today, they will all meet again. A

man covered in tattoos looks at the camera,
he's wearing Amá's eyes; he too must know
the weight of having to carry a hollow space

between his hands. He tells the reporter, *Isn't this the
land where dreams come true?* I want to hold him in
my arms, tell him this is the land where

dreams will destroy you. Another man reminds us
this is a human rights campaign, *Hugs Not Walls.* For
three minutes two countries merge:

Undocumented & México. For seconds
dreams do come true.

III

Amá looks out the car window, traces the border of El Paso bridge with her fingers, *It's been twenty-seven years since I've been this close to the border.* She points to an older man with a sombrero, *Mira, he looks like my father.* She follows the older man with her glance until he disappears in the mix of people walking toward the Santa Fe Bridge.   Amá's eyes shift from side to side, looking for the older man,   she presses her left hand on her chest, & lets out a sigh. In the car   Amá takes the shape of empty; she's been this way for twenty

-seven years. In
September, a letter from Immigration Services   said her Green
Card was approved. Zigzagging up the
Scenic Drive, she stares out the window, she lifts up   her hand,
traces the border that separates El Paso from Juárez,   the mountains
almost hug each other. At the top of Scenic Drive, we stand in front of both countries. The sun wraps her face, reveals her void, I can see the toll that twenty-seven years has taken on her. I put my arms around her, she squeezes my body. *Pronto iré para allá,* she says, extending her arm out beyond the cerros of Juárez pointing at México—

Pronto.

IV

It's December & I stand behind Amá
outside the cemetery gate. The sun sits on
the low east & the only sound near us is

wind. With every step we take toward the gate
her heartbeat pushes her forward, she's here
in her hometown, in her country. I reach for the handle,

she says she can do it. So she pushes & we walk
in. She reads tombstones searching for what she lost
& familiar names remind her she's back, she stops

at each one, leaves traces of her weight. She
continues to read names from tombstones & the
cerros watch her separate her hair from the wind.

All that remains in México is this moment. Two graves down
she finds him. She presses her warm palms against the
blue plaque with the name Genaro Ibarra Parra.

She kneels against him, murmurs: *Aquí estoy, aquí estoy, Papá.*
She keeps glancing at her father's grave & in her words the weight
of her dreams lifting. She grabs my hand & I

squeeze back. I kneel beside her & we become
two cerros leaning on one another looking down at a body
underground covered by dirt, rocks, & a name—

Illusion of Light

The longing for Paradise is man's longing not to be man.

—MILAN KUNDERA, *The Lightness of Being*

Mario's body lies still: pale skin, eyes shut, dreams of
chasing the sun. Mario's face glistens in daylight
the day of his wake. I want to ask him, *Was it that easy to leave
us?* Tía opted for an open casket, so I look at his coffin face,
study his resting smile. *Remember him,* Tía says.
I focus on the speckles of water on his forehead.
The last of what remains of him slides down,

                        drips.

                      ∼

    *Mario. Just call me Mario. Not
Tío, Tío makes me feel old*, he says. Mario who
      uses his hands to cook, to plant, to fix things, to pull
out a lighter from his pocket, turn the flint wheel, create a
      growing spark. & with his other hand, he'd hold a glass pipe:
His mouth would open & he'd inhale heat—Mario,
    who chases the sun, when he's so
        high.

                      ∼

High, high, high—	he chants,
lifting me up	into the sky,
when I point	to the palm trees
around us, I ask:	*How high*
will they grow?	He gargles laughter
in the backyard,	sets me down,

he wipes sweat off   his forehead
with his left arm.   Rays of sun
                                            strike his body.

        I think he's on fire.

                          ～

Through the kitchen window, headlights from a passing car
            strike Tía's torso. She looks outside into darkness,
waits for Mario to appear. She picks up the phone from the kitchen table, dials, asks—
            Is my husband, Mario Martinez, in the hospital?
She spells out his name: *M-A-R-I-O M-A-R-T-I-N-E-Z*,
            Martinez with a Z at the end. She exhales, bows her head, places
the phone down. Cars keep passing by, beams of a lighthouse coming in & out.

                          ～

                          After the funeral, our black attire paints
                          the November sky. In his backyard
                          we stand like his plants: charred
                          with dropped bodies. The freeze from last
                          night took them, too; Tía looks around
                          at the backyard shaking her head:
                          It's like they knew.

The warmth of the afternoon
hits my neck as I walk up
to one of his palm trees &
peel off dead leaves.

                          ～

The call comes
from Tía:
            Mario's dead.
We drive alongside
the night, in the distance

revolving red & blue
lights come into our truck,
a white sheet on
a rolling stretcher.
My youngest cousin
jumps like a sparkler
into my mother's arms when we
get out of the car. We stand outside &
watch the flash of the lights break the sky.

~

At my brother's college graduation party, Mario begs
        me to take him to get more beer. Tía shouts at him:
Haven't you had enough? He laughs & makes a joke,
        Babe, come on. Outside I follow him, he lights a
    pipe & looks up at the sky. Mario who collects stars
in his eyes when he's high.

~

A year after his death, we go through items
in storage. We separate into three different
carts: keeps, donations, & trash. Tía
sees me looking at the only pot she took from
the backyard. She says, *What's losing one more
thing? Take it.* I grab the deep heavy pot, hug it
with both hands, lift with my knees like Mario
taught me, & load it into my car. At home, I
plant a pothos plant inside it & keep it next to
my window. There it grows, reaching
                    &   reaching

~

I remember I found him in the garage two years
before his passing, pieces of an orange ceramic pot
& plants scattered all over the floor.
A bag of fresh mulch & dirt on the table,
an hourglass spilled onto the floor. Mario standing
in the center, stumbling toward me, tossing me the keys,
telling me: *You drive.* I put an arm around him
& I lift him. In the car, he says, *Don't grow up.*
Then, he puts his head outside
the car window, his right arm shoots out too,
grasping the air passing through him.
He laughs whiskey out. I turn to look at him
& I'm blinded by the light in
his face reflecting
into my eyes.

Strand of a Memory

After coming out to my parents
    at 21, I dreamed of suicide.
        It would begin

with the echo of a gunshot,
    a room covered

    in harp wallpaper, my fingertips
        clawing each string

off the walls. My fingers bleed
        out my future.

I see Amá's braided crown
    coming undone. She holds a letter
        with the words *I'm gay. I'm sorry.*

    I find in my hand a thick black strand
        of hair. Amá holding a shotgun,

I tell her, *I'm sorry for pulling your hair.*
    She says, *Yo también lo siento.*
        The bullet's already inside me,

a stream of blood coming out of my mouth.
    Amá asks:
        Where did I go wrong?

        & I'm on the floor already
        in the shape of the word *perdóname.*

This Is How I Fight

I learned how to kiss a man easy
     when he held a gun to my neck. I pulled a thread off my shirt &
        watched the end become a beginning—

At school I was taught how to hide from a storm,
     never how to stop one.

When I was a child, I collected fireflies every night.
     For years I ate them, hoping one day my insides could hold light.

     My therapist asked me today: *Have you forgiven?*

To survive sometimes means to incinerate history.
     Like when Abuelo died, Abuela gathered every single photo from her home,
        cast all the pictures in a metallic tambo & set it on fire.

A man once forbade me to leave the hotel room, *YOU CAN'T GO!*
     I've wondered more than once how lonely you'd have to feel to become violent—

     All through the night he cried, *Why am I not enough?* &
        I bandaged him up with my body.

Afterward, I let water run over me.
     All I heard was static, until

I screamed. I still don't know what hunger
                    is capable of doing.

I keep having a dream of waking up naked
                in my Abuelo's Mexican fields,

lightning has struck everything around me,   a fire is sprouting.

The Dance inside My Abuela

At 13, I saw Abuela Lupe's body
      motionless. Her eyes were closed. I took off my glasses so
            I wouldn't have to see her still. At her velorio
in México, I fell asleep on the bench to the sound
of hymns and prayers.
            That night, Abuela Lupe came to me,
      I'm going to show you a trick. When you die you can
      become anything you want. She said, *Dime en que*
      quieres que me convierta. I asked, *Can you turn into water?*
She said, *Mijo, si agua es lo que somos* & she clenched
her overworked hands, crumpled into a waterfall.
                I found myself submerged
in a pool of water; I panicked, *Abuela! I can't swim.* Abuela said, *I'm going to teach you*
how to float, & her hands pushed my body up to the surface.
There's nothing to be afraid of. I asked Abuela, *Will you always be water?*
         A wave pushes me out, I stand on nothingness. She manifests far from
me & yells, *I can be anything,*
      anything—
        we can be anything, mijo!

      Anything!

Listening for Submergence

The force of running water from outside my apartment rumbles.
I press my hand against the wall, feel the rush. Across town,

a leaking pipe bursts in the middle of the night; my sister wakes
to her heels breaking water on the hardwood floor. She shrieks & Apá

has another dream of his brother's body plunging against
the waves of the Rio Grande. His brother's name overflows Apá's body; he shakes.
I ask him: *How does it feel to drown?*
Answer: *It feels like every single regret is stuck in your throat.*
Outside, it has been raining for a month now. Rainwater accumulates
at the bottom of my apartment stairs,

I watch the deep stream & I wonder if
Jesus knew his feet wouldn't sink when he walked
on the surface of the sea. At home, Amá drinks another glass
of water whenever she sees me, to wash down my gayness.

At night, I fill the bathtub with my body & water pours out,
Amá gulps down another glass of water, my sister's apartment keeps

    leaking, Apá keeps dreaming—

When will this rain end? I ask my sister. She says, *When my floor stops rising.*

& Amá's running out of glasses to drink from, &
    Apá has another dream of his brother's body
        rising in the river: This time Apá jumps in &
            swims toward him. Apá pulls him out & his
                brother's body ascends toward the sky. Apá's face in awe.

This time the water swallows him.

At home, I become obsessed with water.
    I Google: *How many gallons of water can I drink until I drown?*

How to Kill a Goat & Other Monsters

I wish I could start with beauty. Under the snow,
    my ex-boyfriend guns me down, buzzes into my ear:

                Do you know what runs faster than fear?
His hum takes me to Abuelo & me
    in México   dragging   a goat out into snow.

No hoof prints behind us
          only strides of a body in movement.

In the first grade, a boy sees me write his name &
        mine on the last sheet of my spiral with a heart.
During recess, the boys throw my words around,
          pages blow out like baby's breath shaken from their stems.
The boys call me *freak* for the rest of the school year.

My ex-boyfriend's chuckles remind me of those boys,
        he breathes heat into my mouth with the edge of the gun.
           I'm sorry, babe. I just . . . You know how I get.

    & he's right. There's a war in his hands
the way there was a war in Abuelo's hands.
    The war being survival. Survival meaning to eat.

My pomegranate jewels stain the snow crimson.
        My ex-boyfriend bends down, kisses my cheek, brushes his hand
        on my arm, draws circles with his fingers,

        Do you forgive me?

I look at the shiny glare of my blood in the light,
it takes me back to

        Abuelo brushing the goat's belly, laying it down
        against the snow. How Abuelo reached
            into his pocket, took out his navaja.

        Mira, lo tienes que hacer rápido.

Rápido. Fast. A verb of action—That's how I once escaped death
merging onto a highway an 18-wheeler didn't see me
entering. I swerved into the emergency lane.
    Let the monstrous truck pass me by.
        GET UP!

           My ex-boyfriend kicks me
      until I roll in snow sawdust. I groan the way
      the goat did when Abuelo punctured its
      throat.

Te digo un secreto.

  You have to twist the knife

    inside the throat,   *keep twisting it as you pull it out.*

    You'll gut the vocal cords

   it will not be able to shriek.

Before the goat finished bleeding out Abuelo closed its eyes, told it, *Yo no soy un monstruo.*

My ex-boyfriend says,   *Don't be afraid of me. I love you.*

My body can only handle so much love.

When I was seven, I thought I could only find monsters under my bed.
Each night Amá checked under my bed.
After, she'd wrap me in a yellow blanket, *Esto te protegerá.*

Amá forgot to tell me not all monsters can be killed.

Somewhere in the future, snow falls again,
burns my lips like salt.
I'll drag a goat out of my Abuelo's farm.   I'll tell him: *¡Vete! No te quiero matar.*

Because to kill would mean I'm a monster too
& I want to end with beauty.

Notes

The book epigraph is a poem by Sandra Cisneros from *House on Mango Street*.

The lines "*Y volver volver, volver a tus brazos otra vez*" are from the song "Volver, volver" by Vicente Fernandez.

The line "Texas man dies in hospital after car drags him 4 miles" comes from the *Deseret News* article titled "Texas Man Dies in Hospital after Car Drags Him 4 Miles," published in April 2001.

The photo in the poem "Missing Tío" is of my father, whom his family says had similar features as his brother Carlos.

The epigraph of the poem "Water Runs Too" comes from the *New York Times* article "Photo of Drowned Migrants Captures Pathos of Those Who Risk It All," which includes a photo of the bodies of Óscar Alberto Martínez Ramírez and his almost two-year-old daughter Valeria, who were found in the Rio Grande in 2019.

Acknowledgments

Para mis padres, Arturo Alvares Hernandez & SanJuana Hernandez Ibarra—gracias, gracias. You both have supported me through all my dreams. To my siblings, Arturo & Jeanette, thank you for loving me unconditionally. To all my nieces—Adalyn, Raeden, Marissa, Katie, & Lexi, thank you for all the constant laughs & questions. To my sister in-law, Pricilla, who helps my family in many ways, thank you. For Tía Zoraida Ramirez & Tía Cipriana (Lupe) Hernandez, who continue to show me strength. To my cousins, who are like second siblings to me—Chris Ramirez, Desseny Ramirez, Gabina Vasquez, Ingrid Rios, Joanna Vasquez, Julio Hernandez, & Yolanda Ramirez.

To my support system/friends—Alexx Calvo, Teri Castillo, Elizabeth Cevallos, Robert Cevallos, Stefany Cevallos, Bethany Dawson, María Esquinca, Eloy Fernandez, Nina Garcia, Sarah Rafael García, Patricia Garza, Rigoberto González, Victor Guerrero, Gustavo Hernandez, Alexis Hinojosa, Te'Andrea Jackson, Bertha Lopez, Renée Malooly, Susan Masoud, Morgan, Patricia Overton, Khristyn Parra, jj peña, Salena Ramirez, César Ramos, Sara E. Ravell, Elizabeth Rodriguez, Eddie Rosales, Daniela Ruelas, Adrian Ruiz, Rosalino Salgado, Veronica Sanchez, Athena Sevilla, Kevin Strybos, Hernesto Torres, Norma Jean Torres, Alessandra Narvaez Varela, Susan Varghese, & Beatriz Vela, thank you for all the constant laughs, dinners, drinks, walks, & talks. It's a privilege to have y'all in my life.

To my former professors: Rosa Alcalá, Sasha Pimentel, & Jaime Mejía—I cannot express the gratitude I have for all of you. An immense thank you for your consistence support!

To the Macondo Writers' Workshop—Kay Ulanday Barrett, Sherwin Bitsui, Melissa Bennett, Alana Hinojosa, Miguel Angel Ramirez, Monica Rico, Joseph Rios, Angelina Sáenz, Leslie Contreras Schwartz, & Norma Liliana Valdez, thank you for providing insight & guiding me through some of these poems. Most importantly, thank you for giving me a week filled with so much light.

To Tin House Summer Workshop—O-Jeremiah Agbaakin, Ariana Benson, Tianna Bratcher, Chelsea DesAutels, Jena Favinger, Roman Johnson, Dare Williams, & Patricia Smith, I cannot thank y'all enough for a week filled with so much care & love. Thank y'all for believing in my work.

A huge thank you to the editors, managing editors, & readers of the following journals for including earlier versions of selected poems from this book in their publications: *The Acentos Review, Atlanta Review, Blue Mesa Review, Borderlands: Texas Poetry Review, Cherry Tree, Cosmonauts Avenue, Foglifter Journal, Fourteen Hills, Frontier Poetry, The Normal School, Oyster River Pages, PANK Magazine, Pidgeonholes, Pleiades Magazine, Poet Lore, & Quarterly West*. Thank you for giving my poems a space to exist in.

An immense thank you to Kelli Russell Agodon & Annette Spaulding-Convy at Two Sylvias Press for publishing some of these poems as a chapbook, *At Night My Body Waits*, winner of the 2021 Two Sylvias Press Chapbook Prize. A boundless thank you to Victoria Chang for selecting my chapbook as a winner.

Lastly, this book wouldn't be possible if it wasn't for the Wisconsin Poetry Series. A huge shout-out to Sean Bishop, Jesse Lee Kercheval, Jackie Krass, Dennis Lloyd, Sheila McMahon, & Allie Shay; thank you! & thank you to everyone else at the University of Wisconsin Press.

WISCONSIN POETRY SERIES

Sean Bishop and Jesse Lee Kercheval, *series editors*
Ronald Wallace, *founding series editor*

(B) = Winner of the Brittingham Prize in Poetry
(FP) = Winner of the Felix Pollak Prize in Poetry
(4L) = Winner of the Four Lakes Prize in Poetry
(T) = Winner of the Wisconsin Prize for Poetry in Translation

Taken Somehow by Surprise (4L) • David Clewell

Thunderhead • Emily Rose Cole

Borrowed Dress (FP) • Cathy Colman

Host • Lisa Fay Coutley

Dear Terror, Dear Splendor • Melissa Crowe

Places/Everyone (B) • Jim Daniels

Show and Tell • Jim Daniels

Darkroom (B) • Jazzy Danziger

And Her Soul Out of Nothing (B) • Olena Kalytiak Davis

Afterlife (FP) • Michael Dhyne

My Favorite Tyrants (B) • Joanne Diaz

Midwhistle • Dante Di Stefano

Talking to Strangers (B) • Patricia Dobler

Alien Miss • Carlina Duan

The Golden Coin (4L) • Alan Feldman

Immortality (4L) • Alan Feldman

A Sail to Great Island (FP) • Alan Feldman

Psalms • Julia Fiedorczuk, translated by Bill Johnston

The Word We Used for It (B) • Max Garland

A Field Guide to the Heavens (B) • Frank X. Gaspar

The Royal Baker's Daughter (FP) • Barbara Goldberg

Fractures (FP) • Carlos Andrés Gómez

Gloss • Rebecca Hazelton

Funny (FP) • Jennifer Michael Hecht

Queen in Blue • Ambalila Hemsell

How to Kill a Goat & Other Monsters • Saúl Hernández

The Legend of Light (FP) • Bob Hicok

Sweet Ruin (B) • Tony Hoagland

Partially Excited States (FP) • Charles Hood

Ripe (FP) • Roy Jacobstein

Last Seen (FP) • Jacqueline Jones LaMon

Perigee (B) • Diane Kerr

American Parables (B) • Daniel Khalastchi

The Story of Your Obstinate Survival • Daniel Khalastchi

Saving the Young Men of Vienna (B) • David Kirby

Conditions of the Wounded • Anna Leigh Knowles

Ganbatte (FP) • Sarah Kortemeier

Falling Brick Kills Local Man (FP) • Mark Kraushaar

The End of Everything and Everything That Comes after That (4L) • Nick Lantz

The Lightning That Strikes the Neighbors' House (FP) • Nick Lantz

You, Beast (B) • Nick Lantz

The Explosive Expert's Wife • Shara Lessley

The Unbeliever (B) • Lisa Lewis

Radium Girl • Celeste Lipkes

Slow Joy (B) • Stephanie Marlis

Acts of Contortion (B) • Anna George Meek

Blood Aria • Christopher Nelson

Come Clean (FP) • Joshua Nguyen

Bardo (B) • Suzanne Paola

Meditations on Rising and Falling (B) • Philip Pardi

Old and New Testaments (B) • Lynn Powell

Season of the Second Thought (FP) • Lynn Powell

A Path between Houses (B) • Greg Rappleye

The Book of Hulga (FP) • Rita Mae Reese

Why Can't It Be Tenderness (FP) • Michelle Brittan Rosado

As If a Song Could Save You (4L) • Betsy Sholl

Don't Explain (FP) • Betsy Sholl

House of Sparrows: New and Selected Poems (4L) • Betsy Sholl

Late Psalm • Betsy Sholl

Otherwise Unseeable (4L) • Betsy Sholl

Blood Work (FP) • Matthew Siegel

Fruit (4L) • Bruce Snider

The Year We Studied Women (FP) • Bruce Snider

Bird Skin Coat (B) • Angela Sorby

The Sleeve Waves (FP) • Angela Sorby

If the House (B) • Molly Spencer

Wait (B) • Alison Stine

Hive (B) • Christina Stoddard

The Red Virgin: A Poem of Simone Weil (B) • Stephanie Strickland

The Room Where I Was Born (B) • Brian Teare

Fragments in Us: Recent and Earlier Poems (FP) • Dennis Trudell

Girl's Guide to Leaving • Laura Villareal

The Apollonia Poems (4L) • Judith Vollmer

Level Green (B) • Judith Vollmer

Reactor • Judith Vollmer

The Sound Boat: New and Selected Poems (4L) • Judith Vollmer

Voodoo Inverso (FP) • Mark Wagenaar

Hot Popsicles • Charles Harper Webb

Liver (FP) • Charles Harper Webb

The Blue Hour (B) • Jennifer Whitaker

American Sex Tape (B) • Jameka Williams

Centaur (B) • Greg Wrenn

Pocket Sundial (B) • Lisa Zeidner